THE
Archive Photographs
SERIES

AROUND
WALLINGFORD

DI – C

GEORGE V'S JUBILEE, 1935. The Wallingford Rangers won first prize in the decorated motor lorry competition. Standing in the middle row are Olive Emmett and Ethel Rush, whilst Miss Dell and Daisy Wells are two of the ladies sitting on the ground (to the left and centre of the picture).

2

THE
Archive Photographs
SERIES
AROUND
WALLINGFORD

Compiled by
David Beasley

CHALFORD

First published 1998
Copyright © David Beasley, 1998

The Chalford Publishing Company
St Mary's Mill, Chalford,
Stroud, Gloucestershire, GL6 8NX

ISBN 0 7524 1054 7

Typesetting and origination by
The Chalford Publishing Company
Printed in Great Britain by
Bailey Print, Dursley, Gloucestershire

This book is dedicated to the memory of Brian Finch:
a good friend and a gentle man.

Contents

St. Mary's Church & Market Place,.

Wallingford from the Air.

WALLINGFORD MARKET PLACE, LOOKING NORTH, 1920. To the left of the Town Hall is Alfred Wilkin's fruit and vegetable shop, which was demolished in 1936 to make way for a post office. In the centre of the photograph is a white L-shaped building: this was the police station. Opposite the police station, and up a little, are houses that were demolished in 1934 to make way for a cinema.

6

Introduction

In compiling this, my second book of photographs of Wallingford, I had to decide whether to ignore the main events in Wallingford's history which were included in the first book, ie., wars, coronations, jubilees and sundry disasters, or to look for new subjects and fresh information. I decided to take the former course – to miss these events out would be to ignore a vital part of the town's past. A significant factor involved in this decision was the discovery of Gertrude Gardener's 1896/1897 diary, in which she vividly records the day of Queen Victoria's diamond jubilee, initially in Benson and then moving on to Wallingford in the afternoon and evening. This personal record reveals that Victorian sensibilities regarding Queen and Country were very different to the attitudes of the present day.

By collecting many hundreds of cuttings from the *Berks and Oxon Advertiser*, known colloquially as the 'B and O', the full extent of the range of local stories recorded in its pages becomes evident. These range from national matters, such as elections and coronations, to more immediate local issues, such as chimney fires and the number of patients in the local hospital. There are many surprising reports, such as that of a stag being pursued down St John's Road by the hunt and a fox escaping from the hounds in Castle Street by running along the roof tops and down into the Bull Croft. It is of interest to note that, following the former incident, there were a number of letters of complaint in the 'B and O' which condemned the cruelty of stag hunting.

In this worthy journal the great floods of 1894, 1904 and 1927 are recorded, as is the heavy snowstorm of April 1908 and the very high winds that seem to blow up the Thames Valley every few years. The deaths of prominent members of the community have been chronicled. Some of these are very tragic, for example the death of Mary Corner, who drowned herself and her three children in the Thames opposite Howbery Park, following an argument with her husband over money. Similarly pathetic was Nora Marshall's accidental drowning for the sake of her dog, in 1918. The paper also covered events of national significance, such as the introduction of the state pension in January 1909, the Suffragette movement and the general strike of 1926. All these happenings, and many more, are recorded in the pages of this excellent newspaper. During the Boer War and the First World War, the 'B and O' published letters from servicemen. Sometimes this had a tragic aspect when the letter writer was killed before his correspondence appeared in the paper.

My collection of photographs numbers nearly 7,000. The main difficulty in writing this book was deciding which photographs to leave out. In addition to general scenes, which will hopefully appeal to anyone who has even a slight knowledge of the town or an interest in local history, I have endeavoured to include pictures of as many people who have lived, worked and passed their time in Wallingford as possible – this book is their story.

Having lived through the Second World War, I cannot forget those Wallingfordians who were called into the services, many of whom lie buried around the world. The story of the sergeant who stayed with his friend until he died has haunted me all my life. Compiling this book on Wallingford and its people was a labour of love: if it evokes a few pleasant memories for you, then I shall feel it has been a success.

The entrance to the Bullcroft, c. 1930. The German field gun is thought to have been captured during the first World War and was on display here during the 1920s and early 1930s. The pavilion in the background was purchased from Freddie Snow in 1918.

One

The River

ADVERTISEMENT FOR THE GEORGE HOTEL, 1893. This was taken from the *Berks and Oxon Advertiser* of that year. It seems incredible to us today that a bottle of ten-year-old whiskey would cost only 19p.

ENGRAVING OF WALLINGFORD BRIDGE AND GAS WORKS, *c.* 1850. This is by William Willis. The Gaslight and Coke Company of Wallingford was formed in 1834. Street lighting was introduced on Monday 5 January 1835 and a public dinner, entirely cooked by gas, was held at the Lamb Hotel to mark the occasion. The old clock in St Mary's church tower was lit by gaslight and the obelisk that now stands in the Bull Croft, erected in the Market Place at this time, was also illuminated in this way.

WALLINGFORD BRIDGE AND GASWORKS, 1876. This is part of a photograph taken by Henry Taunt. It was the newspaper of the time's considered opinion that this building enhanced the aspect of the area: we can only imagine the protests today if it was decided to build a gasworks on the riverside. When there was an interruption in supply from the new gasworks in Station Road, lasting six weeks, the Corporation reduced the price of gas by ten per cent for a year.

WALLINGFORD TOLL-HOUSE, *c.* 1880. Built in 1819, the Thorpe family were its last occupants when it was finally closed, in 1934. The chimney of the gasworks can be seen in the background of the photograph.

BOSSOM'S WHARF, *c.* 1872. Thomas Bossom, a coal merchant, owned the wharf in front of St Peter's church from 1877 to 1911. The meadow on the right of the picture was, for many years, known as 'Bossom's Meadow'.

WALLINGFORD BRIDGE, LOOKING NORTH, *c.* 1912. Salter's steamers, seen moored on the left, ran a service from Oxford as far downstream as Windsor. Before the First World War, the steamers would often stay overnight in Wallingford, with the passengers staying at the Lamb or the George Hotel and the crew staying at the Temperance Hotel. The meadow on the left was, during the late sixteenth century, the site of Ralph Pollington's weir, which diverted water to the Castle Mills. The building on the edge of the trees is a boathouse, built by J. K. Hedges of Castle House.

OXFORD CANAL WHARF, *c.* 1911. The wharf at this time was owned by Frederick Phillips, a timber merchant related to Joseph Phillips of Crowmarsh. In the 1920s and 1930s, the yard was owned by Frederick's son, George. Barges loaded with timber can be seen moored to the bank, having probably travelled down from Oxford. Any barge passing under Wallingford Bridge would be subject to the toll of a shilling. In the foreground can be seen a crew of Wallingford Rowing Club.

PADDLE STEAMER, THE *JULIA*, MOORED AT OXFORD CANAL WHARF, *c.* 1876.

WATERCOLOUR OF CHALMORE LOCK. Although this was painted in 1911, the picture shows the lock as it would have looked around 1870. In 1867, John Whiteman jnr was the lock-keeper of Chalmore, earning 52s (£2.60) per month, whilst his father was the keeper at Benson. By 1870, the lock was in such a bad state of repair that it was decided that no tolls were to be taken and part of the lock was removed in 1871. There was much opposition to this in the town, as it was thought that lock and weir removal would lower the level of the waterway so much that barges would be unable to negotiate the river. Hilliards at Lower Wharf and Bossom at Canal Wharf both suffered as a result of this.

THE LOCK-KEEPER'S COTTAGE, 1908. This was actually used as the ferryman's cottage and burnt down in the 1920s, when James Shepherd was the incumbent ferryman.

FERRYMAN'S COTTAGE AT CHALMORE, c. 1930. The man in the white cap, in the centre of the photograph, is the ferryman, Mr E. Yates. The cottage was built in 1928 by the Thames Conservancy. On the pillars that support the cottage are two plates that record the flood levels of 1894 and 1947. The ferry was closed in the early 1950s and the cottage is now a private house.

LOWER WHARF, 1876. This photograph was taken by H. Taunt of Oxford. The Hilliard family ran their coal and timber business from this wharf. By 1895, George Corneby was running a boat building business from here. In 1899 Percy Turner bought the wharf. As well as boat building, the wharf was also used for pleasure with boating and swimming being popular here. Note the reeds that can be clearly seen in this photograph: most of the reed beds in the Thames, through dredging and heavy river traffic, have now disappeared – as a result bank erosion has greatly increased as the riverside has no protection.

LOWER WHARF, c. 1925. Percy Turner, the man leaning on a post in the centre of the picture, owned this swimming area. Before 1914, Mr Turner often held concerts – in which he was a major participant – in the building on the right. In 1940 he helped make up the armada of little ships that sailed for Dunkirk to rescue the Allied troops from the beaches.

WALLINGFORD INVITATION REGATTA, 1908. The spectators are seen here on the lawns of Lower Wharf. As well as boat races, a water polo match was held: in the winning team of this event were F.K. Weedon, H. H. Wilder, A. Jenkins, B. Binyon, G. Caudwell, and F. Jenkins. In the men's double-sculls event M. Caudwell, C. Caudwell and Miss M. Curtis (cox), beat W. Dawson, F. Jenkins and Miss D. Peck (cox). The mixed doubles was won by Miss Crook, W. Crook and J. Crook (cox). In the evening a *Cafe Chantant* was held on the lawns, illuminated by the Chinese lanterns which can seen in the photograph. Mr Bert Welfare, of the Reading Pierrots, played from a platform moored mid-stream and, apparently, the group's rendering of *Tickle me Timothy* was very well received.

ADVERTISEMENT FOR THE REGATTA, 1908. Again, this is from the *Berks and Oxen Advertiser*

WALLINGFORD
INVITATION SKIFF REGATTA
WILL BE HELD
On Saturday, August 8th, 1908,
At the LOWER WHARF.

President—James Wilder, Esq., Mayor.
Vice-Presidents—Harvey du Cros, Esq., and Geo.
F. Slade, Esq.

LIST OF EVENTS.

Ladies' Doubles .... entrance		2s.6d.
Gentlemen's Doubles ....:..	,,	2s.6d
Mixed Doubles............................	,,	2s.6d
Scratch Dongola Race	,,	3s.0d.
Water Derby		
Water Polo		

First Race at Two o'clock.

A GRAND CAFE CHANTANT
Will be held at 8 o'clock, at the Lower Wharf,
or if wet at the Rifle Range.
Entries for the Regatta close on August 5th, to
L. F. GALE,
H. H. WILDER, } Hon. Secs.

WALLINGFORD ATHLETIC REGATTA, 1908. This regatta was held to the north of the bridge, two weeks after the Lower Wharf Regatta on the 19 August. The crew in the photograph is in the Goring boat and is comprised of: H. Dodd, (bow), E. Kift, C. Caudwell, H. Tate and C. Beeson (cox). They were the winners of their event. Amongst other winners that year were Miss W. Peck, W. Crook and Miss K. Peck

WALLINGFORD SKIFF REGATTA, c. 1950. This was rowed over much the same course as it is today. Amongst this crew are: Jim Shepherd (bow), Jim Ely (centre), and Aggie Rolls (in the stern). It was near here, in May 1882, that Henry W. Gibbons fell out of his boat at the end of a race and drowned, in full view of the spectators.

ENTRANCE TO WALLINGFORD'S BATHING AREA, *c.* 1935. After over sixty years of discussion, the Town Council finally opened this bathing area in the early 1930s

WALLINGFORD BATHING AREA, 1936. The bathing area was open from May until September. Mixed bathing was allowed daily in two sessions and charges were 3d for adults and 2d for children. The building on the right was the changing rooms and, from here, towels and costumes could be hired for 3d. There was a special area penned off in the river where people were taught to swim: this was usually done by attaching a canvas belt around a pupil's waist which was strapped to a pole held by the instructor, who walked up and down the river bank calling out instructions.

WALLINGFORD POOL, 1956. The pool was opened for the coronation of Queen Elizabeth II in 1953.

CROWMARSH, LOOKING WEST, 1894. The floods, that can clearly be seen in this photograph, later reached as far as the church. In 1809 the flood water had been even higher and a Captain Hilliard was able to row from Calleva House, in the High Street, almost to the Queen's Head before beaching his boat

THE TOWN ARMS, 1894. The flood in March of this year was the second highest recorded on the Thames (only the flood of 1809 was higher). Canal Wharf was submerged under some five to six feet of water and Thomas Bossom and his family had to live upstairs for several days, the water in his house being as deep as two to three feet and in which fish were seen to swim. The flood water reached as far as Edward Morris's china shop on the corner of Thames Street.

LOOKING EAST TOWARDS CROWMARSH, 1947. This was the third highest flood recorded on the Thames. Many of the houses in St Leonard's Lane had outside lavatories which became unusable and residents, such as Tom Robins, had to walk to the public toilet half a mile away. The flood water stretched from the dog-leg of the Thames in the bottom half of this scene to the tree-lined Watery Lane in the top half of the photograph.

THE RIVER AT CHALMORE, MID-WINTER 1927/28. Many people can remember the winter of 1962/63, when the river froze over, but January 1895 was even harsher and temperatures remained as low as thirty-three degrees for twenty-four days. During this spell, a Benson man, named Dearlove, died from exposure and was found by the Henley postman at the side of the road in Nettlebed.

THE LANDING STAGE, c.1945. This photograph clearly shows years of wartime neglect, when little or no dredging of the Thames was carried out. During the Second World War the river around Wallingford was used for the testing of Bailey Bridges by Canadian Engineers and, later, American Engineers who were stationed at Howbery Park. An area to the south of the bridge, where the marina and boatyard are today, was concreted to make three slipways down to the river.

Two

Around Town

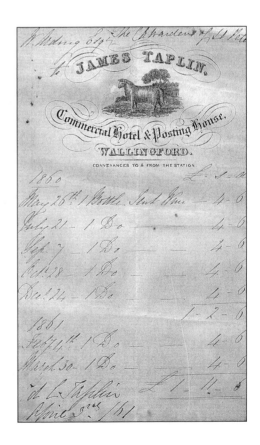

JAMES TAPLIN'S BILL HEADING, THE
LAMB HOTEL, 1860.

THE LAMB CORNER, *c.* 1924. The three-storey building on the left was the house of Richard Deacon. From 1850 to 1885 he was a solicitor at Hedges and Son's. Jane Payne ran a private school here in 1891, until it was moved to Calleva House. The building was converted in the early 1930s and became the premises of Hunt's seed merchants. The building with the Oxo advert in the window was Bruce's grocery store and opposite is Rusher's china shop.

THE HIGH STREET, NEAR THE BULL CROFT, *c.* 1937. The shop with the lady standing in the doorway is John Hoddinott's radio and television business. Television came early to Wallingford: R.J. Wilder was selling Baird Televisor sets as early as 1931. The area from which all the chestnut trees are growing is Harris' builders yard and shop. The next building along is The Beehive public house, the landlord at the time being Cecil Low.

THE HIGH STREET, LOOKING TOWARDS THE KINE CROFT, *c.* 1908. St Albans Priory, the home of John Dazell, is on the left. Nowadays it is the site of Jenkin's garage. In 1902 a tramp was arrested outside St Albans for being drunk. Appearing before the magistrates the next day, he was fined ten shillings. When asked if he had any comments, he declared himself to be happy with the fine as he was charged a pound in Reading a month ago for the same offence.

THE HIGH STREET, NEAR THE KINE CROFT, 1907. Stone Hall, on the left, was the home of Miss Elizabeth Fairthorne between 1860 and 1916: she was more than a hundred years old when she died. In the 1920s, Cavells, wine merchants in Wallingford, were the owners. Next door is Flint House. Nowadays the town's excellent museum it was, in the 1860s, the home of Rowland Atkinson, whose son, William, became a well-known poet and had several books published.

25

THE KEEP, HIGH STREET, 1978. The house was built in 1933 for Dr William Nelson by Smallbones of Streatley. The foundation stone was laid on February 15 1933 by Pamela Hedges, the youngest daughter of Francis Hedges of Castle House. Bricks and timbers from an old barn that was demolished to clear the site were used in the building of the Keep. Dr Nelson lived at Stone Hall until the house was completed.

CROFT ROAD, LOOKING SOUTH, c. 1912. From the High Street to the centre of this photograph, this street was known as Lock Lane until it was developed in 1869.

EGERTON ROAD, LOOKING WEST, *c.* 1908. In 1891, the end house on the right was occupied by John Fowle, a blacksmith, his neighbour being William Crook, a bricklayer. John Mayne lived in the last house.

ST JOHN'S ROAD, LOOKING TOWARD CROFT ROAD, *c.* 1906. The houses on the left were formerly known as Gladstone Villas. In the centre of the photograph is the Plough Inn. George Richard Beale was the landlord for over forty years, from 1881 to 1924.

St. John's Road, Wallingford.

ST JOHN'S ROAD, LOOKING
TOWARDS ST MARY'S STREET, *c.* 1908.
The terraced houses on the left were built by
the local firm of Brasher and Son's, the
white edged design is characteristic of
Brasher buildings. Opposite is the field
where Lord John Sanger often pitched his
circus. Next to the field can be seen St
John's Farm, once owned by the Holmes
family. From the mid 1930s, until it was sold
for housing land in the 1980s, it was owned
by the Bosley's.

ADVERTISEMENT FROM THE *BERKS
AND OXON ADVERTISER,* 1940.

ST MARY'S STREET, *c.* 1907. Coming out of St John's Road, formerly Old Moor Lane, is one of Henry Snow's coal carts. The white houses next to the cart were owned by Brashers, a local building firm. Edgar Brasher himself lived in the second house along whilst Richard Wilder, the iron foundry owner, kept offices next door.

GOLDSMITH'S LANE, LOOKING EAST TOWARDS ST LEONARD'S SQUARE, *c.* 1908. All the houses on the left, as far along as the low white cottage, were demolished in the 1960s. The tower, just off-centre, belongs to a steam laundry, which opened in 1900 with Mr Catt as its manager. On the right is Richard and Henry Wilder's iron foundry, which had opened in 1869. On the corner of Mill Lane, where the Nestle's sign can be seen, is the Ironfounder's Arms, the landlord of the time being William Young. Back in 1870, William Passey, a relation of the scrap dealers from Benson, was the landlord. On the opposite corner of St Leonard's Square is the Rose and Crown.

READING ROAD, *c.* 1902. The sheds behind the trees are soot stores, which collapsed during the snow storm of April 1908. Behind the store can be seen the chimney of the mill owned by Mary Boughton. The garland carried by the children is for May Day. During the eighteenth century the house on the left was used as a grammar school.

READING ROAD, *c*. 1912. The second of these ivy-covered cottages was occupied, in 1891, by Robert Cope, a retired publican. Louisa Preston lived in the third, whilst the first was unoccupied.

ST MARY'S STREET, *c*. 1910. The Coachmakers Arms, the public house on the left, was owned by Daniel Smith – the local name for this establishment was The Rampant Cat. Next door is the premises of Alice Squance, a draper, and then Mrs Emma Holmes, a butcher. The building on the right-hand side is the Royal Standard, of which Joseph Harris was the landlord.

THAMES STREET, *c.* 1909. The white building on the right is Riverside, the home of George Dunlop Leslie, RA. In 1887, to celebrate Queen Victoria's Jubilee, he and James Hayllar presented a life-size portrait of her to the town, which now hangs in the Town Hall. Next door is Coberg Cottage, called Cromwell Lodge today, in which lived a Robert Betteridge, who helped nurse Mary Leslie, George's sister. William Painter, a gardener, lived in the house opposite Riverside.

CASTLE PRIORY, *c*. 1910. After several years of construction, this building was finally completed in 1759. It was built for Judge William Blackstone, a leading legal mind of his day and the author of *Commentaries on the Laws of England*, a book which formed the basis of the American Constitution in 1776. Following eighty years of ownership by the Blackstone family, Thomas Duffield bought the house from W.S. Blackstone in 1848. The house was run by Eliza Large as a boarding school until 1875 when James Hayller, an accomplished artist, purchased it. In 1899, E. Potter became the owner of the house and in 1940 it was acquired by the National Union of Railwayman. After the war it was run as a hotel until 1963 when it was bought by the Spastics Society. Recently the house has reverted into a private residence.

Suffolk House

Boarding Establishment,

WOOD STREET,
WALLINGFORD-ON-THAMES.

Restaurant & Tea Gardens

Conveniently situated in centre of town, ten minutes from Station, two minutes River.

Large and pleasant Garden.

A liberal table supplied, and every endeavour made to ensure the comfort of visitors.

BATHS - (hot and cold).

LUNCHEONS and TEAS.

Large Parties Catered for.

TARIFF ON APPLICATION.

Mrs. LLOYD - - Proprietress.

(and at 14, Market Place).

WOOD STREET, LOOKING NORTH, *c.* 1904. This postcard is actually addressed to George Leslie of Riverside. The first house in the picture is Suffolk House, which was owned by Thomas Pettit, a draper, at this time. In the 1890s Mrs Flora Lloyd, who owned a confectioners in the Market Place, had run a restaurant and boarding house from there. Henry Wilder, the iron foundry owner, lived next door in Lynton House between 1883 and 1911, having purchased the property from Cary Tyso, the famous gardener. The terraced houses that can be seen in the distance were demolished in the 1950s.

ADVERTISEMENT FROM BRADFORDS STREET DIRECTORY, 1910.

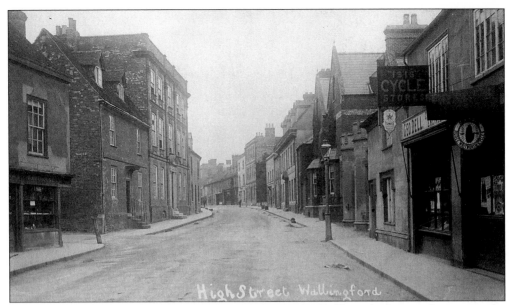

THE HIGH STREET, LOOKING WEST, *c.* 1904. George Dell's cycle shop can be seen on the right, whilst next door lives James Pounsett, a nurseryman, and next along is the residence of Frederick Kirkpatrick, a painter. On the opposite side of the street is Morris's china shop. John Baker, a corn dealer, lived on the corner of Thames Street with Calleva House, a private school, next door. Careful study of the photograph will reveal that the road sweeper has been working his way up the street.

THE HIGH STREET, LOOKING TOWARDS THE BRIDGE, *c.* 1914. Davis and Son moved here from St John's Road in 1913 and by 1920 they had become antique dealers and moved to Calleva House. On the opposite side of the street the first house belongs to John Marshall, a surgeon, next door is owned by Thomas Wells, a brewer, and then comes the house of John Marshall, a solicitor whose daughter, Nora, was well known in the town for her charitable works. This unfortunate girl died tragically in 1918 when she drowned while trying to rescue her dog from the river: ironically, the dog was unharmed.

HIGH STREET, LOOKING WEST, *c.* 1882. The shop with the two boys peering in the window is John Gardener's confectionery store and refreshment rooms. The man in the apron is possibly John Gardener himself. Next door belonged to George Kearsey, landlord of the George Hotel.

ST MARY'S STREET, LOOKING TOWARDS THE HIGH STREET, *c.* 1930. John Bradford's stationers and printing shop can be seen to the right of the photograph. Bradford's also ran a lending library, which began in St Martin's Street and was moved to the shop in 1940. The Kodak sign hangs from Latter's photographic shop and next door is Jenkin's stationery and toy shop: this was once the site of the Wallingford post office and the words 'Post Office' were written in blue and red bricks in the pavement.

THE MARKET PLACE, *c.* 1885. The Corn Exchange, on the left, was built on the site of Mr W. S. Clarke's house in 1856. Franklin and Gale's auctioneers is next door whilst the signboard of William Woodbridge's saddlemaking shop can be seen on part of the same building. The large white building was the home of James Prowse, a wine merchant, with Alfred Marriott, a jeweller, and William Davis, a tea dealer, further along. The building was converted into a Boot's chemists in 1979.

THE MARKET PLACE, *c.* 1925. The film showing at the Corn Exchange is *Puppy Love.* The Corn Exchange was used as a cinema until 1934 when the Regal cinema was opened. George Atkins, a trainee projectionist at the Corn Exchange, remembers the old cans of cellulose film catching fire and having to throw the burning cans out of the window into Little Lane. Franklin and Gale's is still next door, with Frank Jenkin's cycle shop next to it. Wallingford post office, followed by Victor Chadd's tobacconist shop are further along.

ST MARY'S STREET, *c.* 1922. F. E. Bird's shoe-repair shop. Next door is a public house which, over the years, has had various names, including: Farrier's Arms, Railway Arms and the King William VI. Between 1877 and 1883, whilst it was the Railway Arms, Calab Bosley was the landlord.

ST MARY'S STREET, *c.* 1876. The building on the extreme right is Doctor Horne's house. The residence and practice were eventually taken over by his son-in-law, Dr William Nelson (also known as 'Little Nell'), whose wife was a formidable lady. To call the doctor at night, there was a voice tube leading from the front door to the doctor's bedroom, the caller blew up the tube and this operated a whistle at the other end. One night, just after the tired doctor had got into bed, the whistle sounded and the doctor's wife snatched the tube to berate the caller for disturbing them and tell him the doctor was tired, to which came the reply 'Well, perhaps the fellow who's in bed with you could help me, then'. Next door is the Duke's Head public house, pulled down in 1881, William Peyman being the last landlord.

ST MARY'S STREET, c. 1908. On the left can be seen the police station, now the arcade, which was built in 1856 by Moses Winter. It was from the police station that tokens could be obtained for admittance to the workhouse for one night's bed and breakfast in return for a morning spent picking hemp or breaking stone for road repairs. Next door Mr Rushant, a gardener, was a resident for many years. Between Emily Brigenshaw's shop and Mr Rushant's house is the Farrier's Arms, whilst opposite this is the King's Arms, of which Mr Thomas Lucas was the landlord.

St Leonard's Square, Wallingford.

ST LEONARD'S SQUARE, *c.* 1910. The Free Library on the right and the Methodist chapel next to it were both built in 1871. The chapel was constructed on the site of Moses Winter's builder's yard, which had contained a saw-pit. The library was opened by the mayor, Mr Edward Wells, on 4 July 1871. A public half-day holiday was declared for the occasion and members of the Lodge of Odd Fellows and the Court of Foresters formed a procession to the Mayor's house, where they were joined by the Volunteers, the band of the tenth Hussar's, the Corporation and the Free Library committee. They all paraded to the Library where, in front of a large crowd, it was declared open. The white building next to the chapel is the premises of Robert Marsh, a bootmaker.

ST MARTIN'S STREET, 1846. This watercolour was painted by Claude Rowbottom, a local artist. A Waitrose superstore now stands on the site of the malthouse in the centre of the picture.

MALTHOUSES IN NEW ROAD, *c.* 1927. These buildings were demolished in the 1960s when New Road was widened.

THE CORNER OF NEW ROAD AND ST MARY'S STREET, *c.* 1912. Doctor Nelson's house is on the left and the Morris Brother's dairy and fruit shop is next door. The Green Tree public house is the building with the lamp hanging from it. Arthur Giles was the landlord at this time.

Three
The Trade

ADVERTISEMENT FOR FRANK JENKIN'S
GARAGE, 1936. The garage was converted
into a Boot's chemist in 1979.

CRANE AND SHEPHERD'S
LOCAL GROCERY STORE, HIGH
STREET, *c.* 1914. Following Charles
Crane's death, in 1933, Leonard
Shepherd continued the grocery
business until 1950. The shop is now
the Launderama.

RELF'S STATIONERS SHOP,
HIGH STREET, *c.* 1925. George
Pharaoh Relf moved into no. 19,
High Street in 1904, purchasing the
shop from William Beisley, who
moved his watch-making business to
the opposite side of the street.
George Relf married in 1906 and
when he died, in 1914, his wife
carried on the business, selling
mainly toys, until after the Second
World War. At no. 18, W. Davis ran
his second-hand furniture business.
In 1899 these premises were owned
by Henry Norris, a bootmaker, and
his daughter Emily, a straw-bonnet
maker. Robert Gunstone, a
blacksmith whose smithy was in
Wood Street, lived at no. 17.

TOMB'S TEMPERANCE HOTEL, HIGH STREET, *c.* 1908. John Tombs owned no. 21, High Street between 1899 and 1924. He was a prominent member of the Temperance movement in Wallingford for many years.

HOTEL COURTYARD, *c.* 1876. The George probably dates back to the early sixteenth century. Geoffrey Baynton initially called the inn The George and Dragon which, with the passage of time, became abbreviated to the George. The inn's present sign, which depicts George IV, dates back to the 1930s.

SAUNDERS BROTHER'S BUTCHERS SHOP, HIGH STREET, 1905. This photograph was taken at Christmas time. The poster in the centre of the picture is advertising a 'guess the weight of a pig' competition. It is recorded that 389 people entered and a Mr King, of Brightwell, was the winner whilst Mr F. Wells, of Wallingford, came second (his guess being only one pound out) and Mr Witherwell, of Crowmarsh, came third. Between 1891 and 1904 a Scotsman, Robert Kelly, had owned the premises. In 1908 the Saunders sold the business to the Leach brothers, who were also butchers. In 1919 Ben Crudgington, a fishmonger, bought the premises. Nowadays it is an antique shop.

HIGH STREET, LOOKING EAST, *c.* 1908. This is another photograph taken by H. Taunt of Oxford. Walter Hunt, a seed, corn and hay merchant, has his premises on the right-hand side in a building built, during 1900, on the site of Jesse Allright's boot and clothing shop.

THE LAMB HOTEL, 1948. The Lamb was given its name in, or around, the year 1688 by its landlord Silvanus Wiggins. The inn's original name was possibly The Bell. In 1704 a stagecoach service between Wallingford and London was started, although it made little profit as the horses kept dying on the journey. In 1877 James Taplin was the landlord, succeeded in 1883 by Thomas Elliot and then by Jackson Lawrence between 1887 and 1914.

THE LOUNGE OF THE LAMB, 1948. In the centre of the photograph can be seen an old English lacquer clock, made by John Higgs. To the left can be seen a framed genealogy of the Higgs family, who traced their descent back to the reign of Henry II.

STAIRCASE IN THE LAMB, 1948. This was once the courtyard into which coaches drove from the High Street. The Lamb was the headquarters for the local Territorial Army unit and a Masonic Temple Lodge used its facilities. The Lamb was closed in the early 1960s.

CORNER OF ST MARTIN'S STREET AND HIGH STREET, *c.* 1925. Percy Messenger is the man carrying a coat in the centre of the photograph. For many years he was a taxi driver in the town. The shop on the corner belonged to James Rusher and his family who owned the premises from around 1864 until 1939, when it was demolished to widen St Martin's Street. The man at the top of the photograph is a gas lamp lighter and is engaged in trimming the mantle.

HIGH STREET, LOOKING WEST, 1912. The building on the far right belongs to Hilbert Harris, a painter and decorator. His wife, Gertrude, worked as a milliner from the same premises. The Beehive is next door, the landlady being a Mrs Kate Titcombe. Along from this is the old entrance to a row of terraced houses, called Victoria Court, that were pulled down a few years ago. No. 60, the house with the erected sunshade at the far end of the scene, belongs to William Cato, a florist, whilst William Moss, a tailor, owned next door.

REAR OF RED LION COMMERCIAL HOTEL, LOOKING WEST, *c.* 1905. The Red Lion is the building with the tall chimney. In 1823 Thomas Bedford was the landlord and he was replaced by Henry Kirby in 1842. However, by 1847, Mr Kirby had moved on to the Kings Arms in St Mary's Street and James Bowden was running the hotel. He was suceeded in 1851 by William Hector. Around 1869 William Walters took over and he, and then his son Horace, was the landlord until sometime during the First World War. In 1920 a Woolfe Korbetov is listed as being in charge and F. Samon had become the landlord by 1924. Robert Parnell was the landlord by 1931 and Cecil Low moved from Wiltshire to run the hotel in 1934. It closed the following year.

THE CROSS KEYS, *c.* 1870. This watercolour was possibly painted by Robert Cope, the landlord of the pub in the 1870s. His son, Alfred, succeeded him in 1882 when he retired. Alfred remained as landlord until the turn of the century. The Cross Keys is initially listed in the License Register of 1784 and it probably got its name from the old church, St Peter in the West, that once stood opposite, the symbol of St Peter being the crossed keys.

HODDINOT'S RADIO AND TELEVISION SHOP, ST MARY'S STREET, *c.* 1954.

THE MARKET PLACE, LOOKING NORTH, *c.* 1918. Field, Hawkins and Ponking's drapery store is in the centre of the photograph. To the left is the Feathers Hotel, formally known as the Plume of Feathers, of which Mrs Annie Walters is the owner. Next door is John Tomb's ironmongers and then Arthur Tillet's grocery shop.

51

FRANKLIN AND GALE'S AUCTIONEERS, MARKET PLACE, 1906. Franklin and Gale were auctioneers in Wallingford from 1864 until the 1960s. They also owned a cattle market in Wood Street, which is now a car park. Bread oven is the present day occupier of these offices.

WALTER LEMON'S DRAPERY SHOP, c. 1927. This drapers shop is on the corner of Hart Street and St Mary's Street and existed from around 1925 until 1933. The shop was once the Kings Arms public house, which had been closed in 1920. After the Second World War, Henry Lavington had a basket manufacturing business here until the early 1950s.

PETTIT'S SHOP, ST MARY'S STREET, *c.* 1925. This store was established in 1856 by William and Thomas Pettit of Newmarket. Until the First World War the upper storey was used as a dormitory for the shop girls who lived out of town.

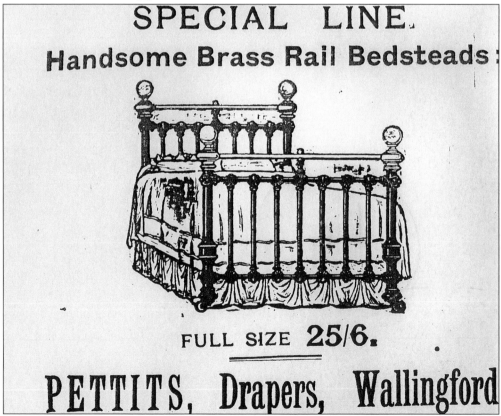

ADVERTISEMENT, 1892. This was taken from the *Berks and Oxon Advertiser*.

EXCERPT FROM PETTIT'S 1906 CATALOGUE.

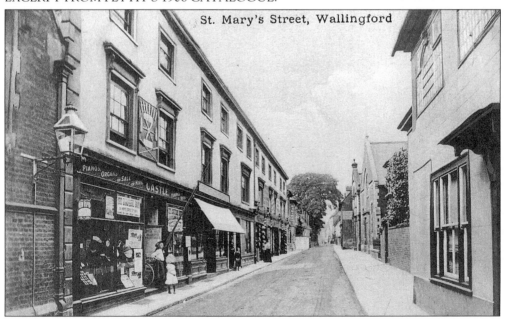

St. Mary's Street, Wallingford

ST MARY'S STREET, 1914. Arthur Castle's music shop is on the left. This shop also sold fireworks all the year round – a display of which can be seen above the shop entrance. Next door was Chamberlain's butchers shop. Behind the white boards in the distance, George Dell's motor shop is under construction. At this establishment in 1914, a motor car could be purchased for £100.

54

Four
The People

BILLHEAD FOR MOSES WINTER OF ST LEONARD'S SQUARE. This bill is for work on St Peter's church and is dated 1860.

DOCTOR EDWIN WALTER, *c.* 1900. Doctor Walter practiced in Wallingford from 1896 until his death in 1932, for the most of the time living in the old St Mary's Rectory (nowadays Barclays Bank) in the Market Place. He served as Mayor from November 1915 to November 1917. At various concerts held in the town he was well known for the singing of comic songs, one of the most popular being *The Old Bachelor*. His son, Arthur, carried on the practice before retiring in the early 1950s.

CYRIL HENSON AND HIS TWO SISTERS, 1916. Cyril Henson lived in Gothic Cottage, St Peter's Street and was the son of Thomas Tyson, the town's registrar for many years. He joined the police force in 1912, later transferring to the C.I.D. and then the Special Branch. He was one of the escorting officers at the trial of Roger Casement. During the 1920s he was a personal detective to George V.

JOHN COPE, c. 1905. John lived at no. 8, High Street from 1879 to 1909 with his wife, Jane, and their nine children, in a three-bedroomed house. He was a coachbuilder and worked for Bowden's of Crowmarsh. During the heat wave of 1909 he collapsed on Wallingford Bridge and died of sunstroke at the age of seventy-seven.

JOHN KIRBY HEDGES BY JAMES HAYLLER, 1890. John K. Hedges was born in 1811, the eldest son of John Allnatt Hedges. He belonged to a family of bankers and solicitors who were very prominent in Wallingford for over two hundred years until Sir John Hedges' death in 1983. John Kirby Hedges was educated at Bedford School before being articled to his father. He eventually succeeded his father as the Town Clerk and, on retiring from practice, he was made a Justice of the Peace for Oxfordshire and Berkshire. At the sale of the Howbery estates, in 1858, he bought the grounds of Wallingford Castle, the 'Castle Banks', where the family house was erected, having already been purchased by his father some years before. The demolition of the house, in 1972, caused a public outcry. Towards the end of the century he wrote his two volume *History of Wallingford* and gave large sums of money to the Cottage Hospital, the Free Library, and the alms houses, as well as paying for a chemical laboratory in the grammar school. In very cold winters he would give £100 worth of coal to the poor of the town. His only son, Launcelot, died in 1878 and the estate was inherited by his three daughters.

ROSEMARY WELLS (NEE HEDGES), c. 1950. Youngest daughter of Francis Hedges, she had one brother, Sir John Hedges, and two sisters, Pamela and Diana. Rosemary married Captain Alfred Wells in 1937 and became a widow in 1940 when Captain Wells was killed in battle in France. She re-married in 1952 to Brigadier King and died in 1974.

NESTA CAVELL, c. 1908. Nesta was the eldest daughter of Percy de Cavell, of Riverside, Thames Street, who was a wine merchant with a shop in the High Street. She married Francis Reade Hedges in June 1910.

THE FIVE DAUGHTERS OF JAMES
RUSHER, c. 1895. The names of the
sisters are: Eliza, Agnes, Ada, Emily and
Minnie. In 1897 Emily married a man
called Charles Matthews. Unfortunately,
in 1899 he was arrested and charged
with bigamy, having been already
married in 1881. The case caused strong
feelings in the town and crowds of some
three hundred people waited outside the
Town Hall during the committal
hearings. The police were so concerned
that they kept Matthews in the building
for over an hour before they took him to
Cholsey Station for the train journey to
Reading gaol. At his trial, Emily refused
to condemn him and stated that she
forgave him, as did his legal wife. The
judge awarded a four-month prison
sentence.

WILLIAM BEISLEY, c. 1896. William
Beisley was a watchmaker living in the
High Street, next door to where the
sports shop is today.

WILLIAM ANTHONY BY A. H. COPE, 1871. The sketch is entitled 'The last night watchman' or 'Charlie' and was given to the Old Wallingford Museum by the artist.

LOCAL POSTMAN, *c.* 1905. This is possibly a member of the Blisset family of St John's Road. Postmen's hours of work were from 7.30 am until 9.00 pm. It used to be possible to post a letter in Wallingford at nine o'clock in the morning and expect it to be delivered anywhere within the town by noon.

JAMES HAYLLAR BY EDITH HAYLLAR, 1890. Edith Hayllar painted this picture of her husband to supplement a series of portraits of local dignitaries that he carried out in 1890 and 1891, which can now be seen hanging in the Town Hall.

HENRY HAWKINS BY JAMES HAYLLAR, 1889. Henry Hawkins came to Wallingford from Andover in 1850 to work as a mercer for Thomas Field, who owned the draper's shop in the Market Place. In less than ten years he came to be a partner in the firm. He was elected to the Council in 1862. In 1880, because some councilors expressed qualms regarding the secrecy of ballot papers used in past Town Council elections, he burnt the previous six year's papers in their presence in order to remove any doubts they may have had concerning the confidentially of the votes.

FREDERICK WILKINS, *c.* 1908. Federick worked as a butcher's delivery boy for Mrs Emma Holmes's shop at no. 39, St Mary's Street. The photograph was taken in Egerton Road by J.A. Latter.

THE SCOUT PLAY, TEMPERANCE HALL, 1909. On the left is C. Brasher, playing Silver Fox, and on the right is B. Curtis, playing Eagle Wing, in a production of *Pocahontas*.

Five

Church, Education and Recovery

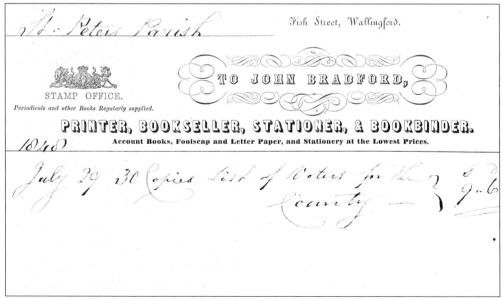

JOHN BRADFORD OF FISH STREET, BILLHEAD, 1848. Fish Street was later to become St Mary's Street.

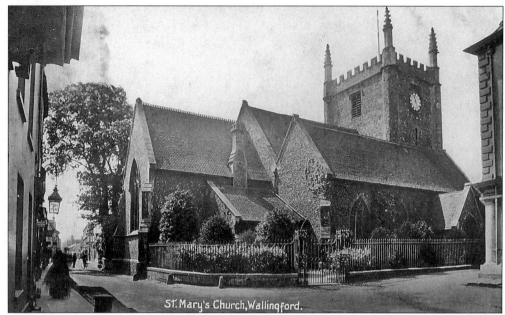

ST MARY'S CHURCH, 1912. Much of this building had been taken down and rebuilt in 1854. The tower had been severely damaged in 1638 and rebuilt in 1653 by William Loader, the materials for this probably coming from the castle which was demolished in 1652. The pinnacles, now removed, were erected as a sign of the town's loyalty to the monarchy during the Restoration. The lamp on the left is hanging from the post office.

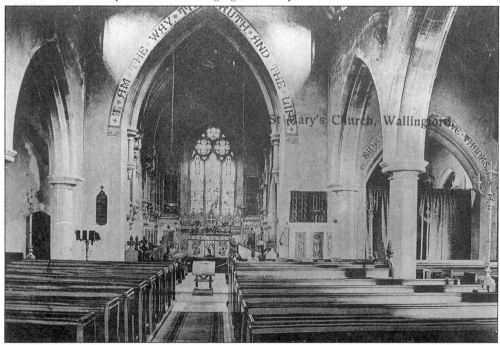

ST MARY'S CHURCH, INTERIOR, c. 1910. This photograph was taken before the rood screen was erected. The organ was originally in a gallery above the altar and was moved to the west gallery a few years later.

LAYING THE CORNER STONE OF WELLS MEMORIAL CHAPEL, 1911. The Wells Memorial chapel is at St Mary's church and this event took place in March. The chapel was erected in the memory of Edward Wells, a churchwarden for sixty-six years. The men on the right are Freemasons from St Hilda's Lodge, Wallingford, of which Edward Wells was a member. The rector, Canon Deacon, is the churchman in the picture scratching his head.

ST LEONARD'S CHURCH, *c.* 1876. During the English Civil War this church was used as a barracks and left as a ruin, but managed to escape the complete destruction suffered by St Peter's and All Hallows' churches. In 1685 repairs to the church began and it was open for divine service by 1704. In 1850 the small wooden bell turret was replaced with the stone tower and a new south isle was built.

ST LEONARD'S CHURCH, INTERIOR, *c.* 1876. The pillars on the right replaced the old piers when the church was restored in 1850. The church is in St Leonard's Lane, which was known as Little Fish Street around 1800.

ST PETER'S CHURCH, *c.* 1924. The church was rebuilt in 1760, over a century after its destruction by Parliamentary forces during the civil war. In 1775 the spire was added and Mr William Blackstone paid for a clock face that faced his bedroom in the Castle Priory, so he could see what the time was whilst still lying in bed. A monument to William Blackstone, at the entrance to the family vault, can be seen on the south side. A chancel and a vestry were added in 1904.

WALLINGFORD GRAMMAR SCHOOL, 1875. The school was opened on 10 September 1877 by Edward Wells, MP. Additional class rooms were added in 1902.

CALLEVA HOUSE SCHOOL,
WALLINGFORD.

DANCING CLASS

Will begin on Monday, 5th October. A Saturday Class is also proposed.

MISS CROSS will be pleased to enrol names of Boys and Girls wishing to join these Classes.

WALLINGFORD GRAMMAR SCHOOL FOR BOYS AND GIRLS.

Scholarship.

ONE SCHOLARSHIP, open to boys and girls, giving free tuition at this School, will be awarded on the result of an examination to be held at the School on Saturday, October 3rd, at 10 a.m.

Candidates must be OVER 12 years of age and UNDER 13, and must have been for two years previously at a Public Elementary School. Applications, addressed to the Headmaster, the Grammar School, Wallingford, marked "Scholarship," must be sent in, on or before Friday, October 2nd.

WALLINGFORD GRAMMAR SCHOOL ADVERTISEMENT, 1908. This advertisement is for scholarships and evening classes at the school and was placed in a September edition of the *Berks and Oxon Advertiser*.

ST ANTHONY'S SCHOOL, GIRLS IN PT LESSON, *c.* 1928. Members of staff at the school included: Miss M. Hedges, Miss K. Trafford, and Miss M. Carnell. The school finally closed in the late 1940s. In the background of this photograph the ruins of St Nicholas College can clearly be seen in the castle grounds.

Opposite: CLASSROOM IN ST ANTHONY'S SCHOOL, *c.* 1928. This school was located off the High Street and was accessible via a narrow lane running between nos 74 and 75. A rear entrance from Bear Lane also existed. The school was run by Miss Violet Hedges and one of its most famous pupils was the actress Dulcie Grey. In 1926 the school put on a production of Hans Christian Anderson's *The Tinder Box*: amongst the players were Dulcie Grey, Daphne McMullan, Rosemary Hedges, Pamela Hedges, Kenneth Saxby, Alison Bowen, Nancy Rudkin and Oliver and Nigel Bowen.

KINE CROFT SCHOOL, JUNIOR GIRLS, *c.* 1920. This school was erected in 1861 at the cost of £2,000. In 1920 Miss Bessie Lovejoy was the headmistress of the school and Mrs Lillian Meredith was the teacher in charge of the infants.

ST JOHN'S SCHOOL, JUNIOR BOYS, 1948. From left to right, back row: Richard Lay, Peter Wright, Allan Coles, Mike Abbot and Dave Mills. Middle row: Freddie Hossick, Michael Whale, Peter Eldridge, John Davis, Bernie Atkins, Billy Batten, Dave Beasley, Jimmy Abbot, Brian Tilly and Dougie Sheard. Front row: Peter Shayler, Peter Sheradan, Peter Bucknell, John Chedsey and Allan Pemberton.

CLIFFORD ATWELL, HEADMASTER OF ST JOHN'S SCHOOL, *c.* 1948. Pictured here in his study.

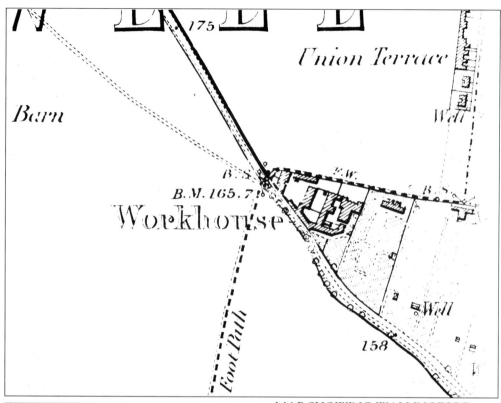

MAP SHOWING WALLINGFORD WORKHOUSE, 1876. This is a part of the Ordinance Survey map showing the Wallingford Union workhouse. The first workhouse in the town was started in 1782. A new workhouse was built in 1834 following the introduction of the Poor Law Act. The map shows the workhouse as it was originally built. The areas of open field represented on this map are now all built upon.

WORKHOUSE, WANTAGE ROAD, c. 1954. This is the workhouse receiving room where the men and women were separated.

ISOLATION HOSPITAL, ST GEORGE'S ROAD, *c.* 1909. The hospital was built in 1904 on land bought from the Park Farm estate. There was much opposition to the building of the hospital, despite an outbreak of typhoid fever in Cholsey in 1893. The top of Crowmarsh Hill was considered as an alternative site.

ISOLATION HOSPITAL, 1910. This photograph shows the building after it was struck by lighting in April 1910. The force of the strike was so great that the floorboards on the landing and first floor bedrooms were driven through the ceiling, leaving some two to three feet of timber protruding.

MORRELL'S MEMORIAL HOSPITAL, READING ROAD, *c.* 1908. Built in 1881, the land for the hospital was given by Henry Hawkins and the buildings provided by Mr and Mrs G. H. Morrell. The hospital was named after Miss Mary Morrell of Whitecross, who died in June 1880. The hospital had eight beds, with living quarters for a matron and a nurse and was supported by voluntary contributions.

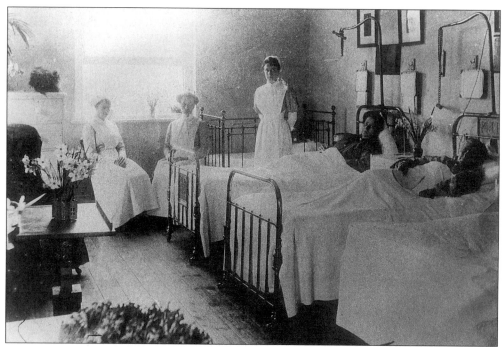

LADIES' WARD, MORRELL MEMORIAL HOSPITAL, *c.*1906.

OPENING OF THE COTTAGE HOSPITAL, READING ROAD, 1929. The hospital was opened in July by Mrs Herbert Morrell. Dame Clara Butt, of North Stoke, sang after the official opening ceremony had been completed

GREAT WESTERN RAILWAY TIMETABLE, 1894. This was the special timetable for the Oxfordshire Agriculture Show, held in Mongewell Meadows.

THE WALLINGFORD BUNK RETURNING FROM CHOLSEY, *c.* 1940.

WALLINGFORD RAILWAY STATION AND GOODS YARD, 1940. In the late 1950s, when passengers were scarce, Percy Norris, who doubled as ticket collector and signalman, was known to hold up the train until a regular passenger arrived. Hidden among the trees in the background is St Mary's Rectory (now the Rectory Garage).

Six

Coronations, Jubilees and Pageants

ADVERTISEMENT FOR EDWARD VII'S CORONATION, 1902. This was taken from a May edition of the *Berks and Oxon Advertiser*.

MARKET PLACE, 1887. It is the 21 June and the Jubilee procession is passing the Feathers Hotel. At the head of the parade is the town band, followed by the local volunteers under the command of Sergeant Payne and then the police, lead by Superintendent Borlase. The Mayor, W.R. Powys-Lybbe, is wearing his new official robes amongst the town council, who are following the police. Bringing up the rear are the members of the Odd Fellows and Foresters, attired in their sashes.

HIGH STREET, 1897. Queen Victoria's Diamond Jubilee on 22 June. The weather for this occasion was very sunny, indeed such conditions were known as 'Queen's weather', because it always seemed to be fine on royal celebrations during her reign. The bridge is covered with chinese lanterns and fairy lights

CHILDREN'S JUBILEE TEA PARTY, 1897. At one o'clock a public lunch was held for all men and boys over fourteen years old. The children were given tea at five o'clock whilst the ladies seem to miss out on both lunch and tea. After the tea, all children were presented with a Jubilee mug by the Mayoress, Mrs Ponking.

KINE CROFT, JUBILEE SPORTS DAY, 1897. One of the highlights of the sports was the churchwardens' race. Halfway through this event the competitors were required to light a long clay pipe and return with it smoking. The race was won by William Turner; F. Blackwood came second. In her diary of that day, Gertrude Gardner records that, on leaving the Water Carnival, she could see the beacon fires fading in the hills around Wallingford. She reckons it to be one of the happiest days of her life and the most memorable day England would ever see.

Opposite: CHILDREN'S JUBILEE TEA PARTY, 1897. The Mayor, Henry Ponking, can be seen talking to the children on the left and, on the right-hand table, the Jubilee mugs can be seen. The town hall is behind the table on the right and on the left is Franklin and Gales, the auctioneers (now the Bread Oven). After the tea there was a decorated-cycle parade, won by A.C. Arding, followed by a water carnival.

WALLINGFORD PROCLAMATION OF EDWARD VII, 1901. The proclamation was given on 25 January. It was read by the Mayor, Thomas Pettit, and attended by the town clerk, Mr F.E. Hedges, the mace bearer, Mr W. Blackwood, and as many of the Corporation as could get on the balcony. The rector of St Mary's church arranged for all the schools to close so that the children could attend the event.

ST MARY'S STREET, GEORGE V'S
CORONATION, 1911. On the left of the
photograph is the drapery store, of which
John Simmonds was the manager. Next
door are the offices of the *Berks and Oxon
Advertiser*, owned by Daniel Jenkins.
Millward's shop is the next building and the
White Hart is the public house with the flag
that is draped across the road.

KINE CROFT, CORONATION SPORTS
DAY, 1911. In one of the marquees behind
the children watching the events, a baby
show was held for all babies born after
George V's accession: there were sixteen
entrants. Mrs Bill Castle's baby was the
winner, Winifred Hobb's progeny won
second prize, Mrs J. Wood's child took third
and the fourth place went to Alice May
Eldridge.

HIGH STREET, GEORGE V'S CORONATION, 1911. The Mayor, Sidney Hawkins, appealed to the inhabitants to decorate and illuminate their homes. The enthusiasm of Wallingford's response to this can be seen in this photograph. Field, Hawkins, Ponkings, and Calleva House were all decorated with large quantities of flowers, whilst evergreens were used at the premises of Dr Nelson and Dr McMullen. The most colourful spot in town was thought to be the south end of St Mary's Street.

BOROUGH OF WALLINGFORD

JUBILEE PROGRAMME

Monday, 6th May, 1935

7.30 a.m.	**BELLS** will be rung from St. Mary's Church.
10.30 a.m. to 10.55 a.m.	**THANKSGIVING SERVICE** IN THE BULL CROFT, IF FINE, IN THE CHURCHES AND CHAPELS IF WET. All are invited to attend and are requested to take their places. The Mayor and Corporation accompanied by the Territorials will arrive at 10.25 a.m.
2–4 p.m.	**SPORTS** IN THE BULL CROFT. These have been arranged so that all may take part. Prizes will be given. Full particulars and entries to Mr. R. Nicholls, 8 Springdale.
2–4 p.m.	**FREE CINEMATOGRAPH ENTERTAINMENT** AT THE REGAL CINEMA. For Children residing in the Borough and attending School. Tickets will be issued to Elementary School Children at the Schools. Tickets for other Children obtainable from the Hon. Secretary.
4 p.m.	**CHILDREN'S TEA** AND PRESENTATION OF MUGS (kindly given by the Mayor). In the Masonic Hall immediately following the Cinematograph Show. Tickets for the Tea (including gift of mug) to be obtained as above-mentioned.
4 p.m.	**UNEMPLOYED'S TEA.** For persons residing in the Borough. In the Conservative Hall. Tickets to be issued by the Labour Exchange.
4.30 p.m.	**OLD PEOPLE'S TEA.** For people aged 70 years and upwards. In the Methodist Hall, St. Mary's Street. Tickets from the Rev. F. S. Collison, St. Mary's Street.
	FOR OLD PEOPLE UNABLE TO ATTEND THE TEA a gift of either Tea or Tobacco will be delivered by Members of the Committee.
5 p.m.	**CARNIVAL PROCESSION.** ENTRY FREE. PRIZES WILL BE GIVEN. Entrants to be at the Bull Croft by 5 o'clock for Judging and at
6 p.m.	LEAVE BULL CROFT and parade around the Town.
8 p.m.	**H.M. KING GEORGE V'S BROADCAST FROM BUCKINGHAM PALACE** will be broadcast from the TOWN HALL

ADVERTISEMENT FOR GEORGE V'S SILVER JUBILEE, 1935. This was printed in a May edition of the *Berks and Oxon Advertiser.*

THE MARKET PLACE, JUBILEE DAY, 1935. On the balcony is the Revd H.P. Bowen, Francis Hedges, (the town clerk), Mayor Harold Lovelock and Horace Walters. The Mayor is about to start the procession to the Bull Croft. On the left can be seen Frank Jenkins' garage, with the post office the adjacent premises.

THE BULL CROFT, 'TUG-OF-WAR' EVENT, JUBILEE CELEBRATIONS, 1935. The team featured in this photograph are the Territorials, who were defeated by Wilder's. The team includes: Cyril 'Basher' Beasley, Harry Edwards, ? Moss and George Strudwick, whilst the anchorman is Fred Lovegrove. The team-member in the skirt belonged to the football team, who all played wearing skirts. On the left, watching the pull, is Bill Soden, with Mr Giffin in the cap next to him.

CHILDREN OF BRITISH LEGION MEMBERS' OUTING, 1948. The children are being taken to the cinema as a Christmas treat. Amongst the children are Sammy Griffin, Peter Harris, Peter Baber, Mike Woodley, Dickie Palmer, Dougie Sheard, Dave Beasley, Mike Cox, George Digweed, Peter Lee, Tony Crabbe, Janet Illes, John Jeskins, Robert Crook, Margaret Crook, Dave Richards, Valerie Palmer and Peter Wells.

CASTLE GROUNDS, FESTIVAL OF BRITAIN CELEBRATIONS, 1951. For this event the North Berkshire drama guild held a masque in the Castle Grounds. The Sinodun Players, the Barn Theatre Group of Didcot, the A.E.R.E. drama society and children from the schools of Wallingford each performed a scene depicting the founding of the town. These maypole dancers are from Wallingford County girl's school and were trained by Daisy Rowe.

CASTLE GROUNDS, FESTIVAL OF BRITAIN CELEBRATIONS, 1951. Another scene from the masque. More than seventeen hundred people attended the performance and it was a considerable success. The script was adapted from one lent by Cifford Atwell. John Morley was the overall producer and he was assisted by Francis Curtis.

HODDINOTT'S ELECTRICAL
SHOP, ST MARY'S STREET, 1953.
The shop is decorated for the
coronation of Elizabeth II.

ST MARY'S STREET,
CORONATION DECORATIONS,
1953. The Salter's Steamers sign to
the right is hanging from Michael
Latter's photography shop. Next door
is Arthur Jenkin's toy and stationery
shop.

ST MARY'S STREET, CORONATION PROCESSION, 1953. The lady in the St John's uniform is Olive Robinson (nee Emmett) and the boy standing next to her is her son, Peter. Dora Kimber is standing behind them whilst Stan, her husband, is seated with their daughter, Eilleen, who is wearing a crown.

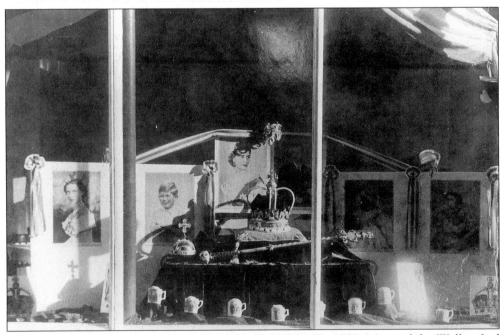

WINDOW DISPLAY, COPPER KETTLE RESTAURANT, 1953. Many of the Wallingford shops exhibited things in their window display which were not normally sold in the shop, for example, a sea shell in a clothes shop window. There was great competition amongst the children of the town to spot all these strange items.

CAKE FOR THE WALLINGFORD OCTOCENTENARY, 1955. In August 1955, Wallingford celebrated its existence as a borough for 800 years. There were many forms of celebrations, the height of which was a pageant, depicting scenes from Wallingford's history, held in the castle grounds. The BBC broadcasted one of the perfomances. A tea party was held in the Market Place for all of the town's children and this celebration cake was divided amongst them.

TOWN HALL, OCTOCENTENARY CELEBRATIONS, 1955. This is a scene from the tea party. Among the crowd, from left to right, are Ruby Day, Kath Hoar, Grace Tubb and Edna Kiddie. Ted Wells is behind the microphone.

CHILDREN'S TEA PARTY, 1955. Over seven hundred children attended this tea party, which was held on a very hot day. The Mayor, Councillor J.O. Johnstone, was accompanied by the Mayor of Wallingford, Vermont, USA, Mr Jerome Johnson. After the tea, the children were entertained in the Kine Croft, with a Punch and Judy show and conjuring.

WALLINGFORD PAGEANT, 1955. Mrs Tot Simmonds, her son David and 'Basher' Beasley waiting to play their parts.

SCENE FROM THE PAGEANT, 1955. This depicts Colonel Fairfax surrendering Wallingford castle to the Parliamentary forces in 1646. The bent figure at the front is a wounded cavalier, played with much pathos by Martin Whillock. After the last performance of the pageant, there was a torchlight procession to the Kine Croft for a bonfire and firework display which some twelve thousand people attended.

SCENE FROM THE PAGEANT, 1955. The children in this scene were: Caroline Bosley, Jennifer Tappin, Rosemary Lester, Patsy Head, David Nunn, Frankie Feast, Martin Whillock, Bob Elliot, David Beasley, John Jeskins, Johnnie Hobbs, Clive Hobbs, Josie Childs, Martin Crossky and Tim Wilder.

Seven

Pleasure

DO NOT FORGET TO LOOK FOR
THE BRITISH WOMEN'S TEMPERANCE
TEA TENT IN THE FAIR.

BOROUGH OF WALLINGFORD.

THE MICHAELMAS FAIR.

NOTICE IS HEREBY GIVEN, that the above Fair will be held until further notice in a place called the KINE CROFT and IN NO OTHER PART OF THE SAID BOROUGH.

Vans, Show Carts, and Roundabouts, will be allowed to enter the Town and proceed direct to the Kine Croft after six o'clock in the evening of FRIDAY, the 28th day of SEPTEMBER instant, but will not be allowed to remain in the Kine Croft or Town after EIGHT o'clock in the fore-noon of TUESDAY, the 2nd day of October next.

Proprietors of Shooting Galleries and others must not leave any broken glass or crockery upon the ground.

The use of squirts and such-like things at the Fair is strictly prohibited, and instructions have been issued to the Police accordingly.

Dated this 4th day of September, 1906.
GEORGE F. SLADE, Mayor
FRANCIS E. HEDGES, Town Clerk.

ADVERTISEMENT, 1906. This comes from the *Berks and Oxon Advertiser*. The town seemed to have had great difficulty in moving the Michealmas Fair from the Market Place to the Kine Croft, as a similar advert had appeared in the paper in 1894.

THE MARKET PLACE, MICHEALMAS FAIR, *c.* 1900. Farm workers and servants were hired at this event. If a man or a lad was for hire, he would wear an appropriate symbol in his cap, i.e, a piece of wool for shepherds, whipcord for a horseman, etc. Once he had been hired he wore a bunch of bright ribbons. Headley's stationery shop and the Feathers Hotel can be seen in this photograph.

MICHEALMAS FAIR, BOTTLE-SHOOTING GALLERY, *c.* 1900. On these occasions the Market Place would be crowded with Bird's and Bailey's galloping horses, several shooting galleries, stalls selling sweets and stalls selling sausages – where the cry of 'one and bread' would be heard. At dusk it would all be lit by electric light. It may have been great fun, but the noise from the steam engines generating the power would be a great nuisance to those living around the Market Place. Some of the older inhabitants must have longed for the return of horses, despite the smell and mess.

MICHEALMAS FAIR, BOXING BOOTH, *c.* 1900. This photograph shows the Market Place, looking east. One of the novelties at the fair of 1894 had been a demonstration of American baseball. A local newspaper had described this sport as one that involved shying a ball at a live man's head.

WALLINGFORD FAIR, LOOKING NORTH TOWARDS THE HIGH STREET, *c.* 1952. In the years following the Second World War, the whole town seemed to go to the fair and it was indeed a family occasion.

WALLINGFORD CRICKET CLUB, *c.* 1908. From left to right, back row: P.R. Latter (Honorary Secretary), W.G. Walters, E. Walters, W. Perrin, F. Frewin, W. Lester and H. Soper (Treasurer). Front row: T Cox, H. Munday, V. Pitt, P. Saunders, E. Stallwood, J. Stevens and ? Pitt.

WALLINGFORD WEDNESDAY SWIFTS, 1908/1909. The team was: (goalie) J. Steel; (backs) P. Beale and S. Millard; (half backs) F. Hedges, R. Gibbons and E. Freeman; (forwards) T. Winfield, W. King, J. King, J. Freeman and H. Harvey.

WALLINGFORD TOWN FC, 1953. This photograph shows the team being introduced to the Mayor of Wallingford, Councillor Johnson. As part of the coronation celebrations, Wallingford played the amateur side, Pegasus, from Oxford. Peagus were very famous at this time as they had won the F.A. Amateur Cup. The team, from left to right: Bert Butcher (captain), Charlie Soden, D. Gomm, ? Green, Dickie Palmer, Johnny Low, Siddy Warwick and ? Lee (goalkeeper).

WALLINGFORD TOWN v PEGASUS, 1953. Bert Butcher gets his man

WALLINGFORD ATHLETIC CLUB GYMKHANA, JUNE 1909. The decorated bicycles event was won by Miss M. Curtis. Miss Henson came second and third was Miss Betty Freeman.

WALLINGFORD GYMKHANA, JUNE 1908. The gymkhana took place in the Paddock, St John's Meadow on a Wednesday afternoon. Despite being held on a working day, over a thousand people turned up.

WALLINGFORD GYMKHANA, 1908. The bicycle obstacle race. This was won by Arthur Jenkins.

WALLINGFORD GYMKHANA, 1905. The decorated bicycle competition. The winner in this particular year was Miss D. Wilder with the second prize going to Miss D. Peck. Miss M. Curtis came in third place.

WALLINGFORD GYMKHANA, 1905. The ladies' push-ball competition. Although push-ball is not a sport that we associate with Edwardian gentlewomen, the gymkhana also had more traditional feminine events, such as the skipping race, won by Bessie Crook, and the bouquet race, won by Miss Deacon.

WALLINGFORD GYMKHANA, 1908. The tilting the bucket competition. In this event a competitor had to push a wheelbarrow with their partner sitting in it, holding a pole. The object of the game was to put the pole through a small ring, attached to a bucket of water suspended over a frame, without spilling the water. Judging by this photograph, the manoeuvre was not always successful! The winner of this race was Leonard Gale and G. Holmes. Arthur Jenkins was one of the pair who came second.

WALLINGFORD QUOITS TEAM, *c.* 1906. Amongst these players are W. Castle, J. Norris, W. Fletcher, H. Gill, W. Nunn, W. Pyke, J. Hedges, A. Williams and P. Beale

WALLINGFORD JAZZ
BAND, 1925. Left to right:
B. Moody, R. Dearlove, H. Ely,
E.H. Pyke.

WALLINGFORD BOY SCOUTS, *c.* 1909. This detachment was formed in late 1908. Mr Youngman was the Scoutmaster. The corps was about thirty strong and had its headquarters at St Mary's church house. They gave their first public show in 1909, which consisted of a demonstration of scouting skills and a short play called *Pocahontas*.

WALLINGFORD GIRL GUIDES, *c.* 1925. This photograph was taken at Moulsford. From left to right, back row: Louis Brown, Beatrice Paxford, Iris Povey, Jenny Last, Brita Smith. Front row: ?-?, Molly Taylor, Captain Lawrence, Lousia Green, Nellie Strange.

WALLINGFORD CARNIVAL, JULY 1930. Field, Hawkins and Ponking's second float, passing along St John Road. Other prizewinners were Keith Jenkins and A. Dunsden for the best-decorated private vehicle, Mrs M. Whiteley for her decorated pram and Miss Pamela Hedges for her fancy dress. The children's prize went to Dolcie Bosley.

PETTIT'S PRIZEWINNING PEDESTRIAN FLOAT, 1930. Although the carnival was held on a Wednesday, over three thousand people were able to attend it.

WALLINGFORD CARNIVAL, 1930. The Old Woman who lived in a shoe. Other exhibits included a huge Platinum pen and pencil, a castle with living toy soldiers, and an airship.

ST MARY'S CHURCH, c. 1920. The town councillors leaving the church on Mayor's Sunday.

BOYS' BOXING MATCH, CASTLE GROUNDS, *c.* 1938. In the years prior to the Second World War, Wallingford had its own boxing club, which had been formed in February 1938. Matches were held against Abingdon boxing club, the Territorials and Turner's Court.

VICTORY CELEBRATIONS, 1945. This photograph shows Peter Baber and Brian Whale taking part in the festivities.

WESSEX ELECTRICAL COMPANY PARTY, CHRISTMAS 1948. This was held in the town hall. The company was later to form part of the Southern Electricity Board. The children, from left to right are, front row: ? Hammond, ? Hammond, R. White, Crissy Thomas, ?-?, David Beasley, ?-?, ?-?, Christopher Aves. Second row: Peter Wright, Dave Thomas, ?-?, ?-?, Judith White. Third row: ? Kiddie, ?-?, ?-?, ?-?, Brenda Soden, Lance Kiddie, ?-?, M. Farmer, ?-?, ?-?, Jean Beasley, Wendy Beasley.

WESSEX STAFF, CHRISTMAS PARTY, c. 1950.

WALLINGFORD RIFLE CLUB, *c.* 1952. The club met in an old nissan hut on what was locally known as 'The Concrete' (now the local marina). Mr John Wilder is the man about to take a shot. Watching him are, from left to right: ?-?, Jim Pink, ?-?, ? Honeybone, Tim Wilder, Bill Moore, Ted King, Wally Emery, Allan Horn, Charlie Gard, ?-?, ?-?, ?-? and Joe Eversley.

WALLINGFORD PANTHERS CYCLE SPEEDWAY TEAM, *c.* 1954. The four riders are, from left to right: Alan Coles, John Whale, Billy Batten and Derek Belcher. The man holding the cup is 'Tanker' White, who built and repaired the bicycles.

HAROLD MACMILLAN, CASTLE GROUNDS, *c.* 1954. Harold MacMillan is opening a Conservative party fete. The man with his hand raised to his mouth is Sir John Hedges.

DUKE OF EDINBURGH REGIMENT, 1995. This is their final march past before being disbanded.

Eight

Military Matters

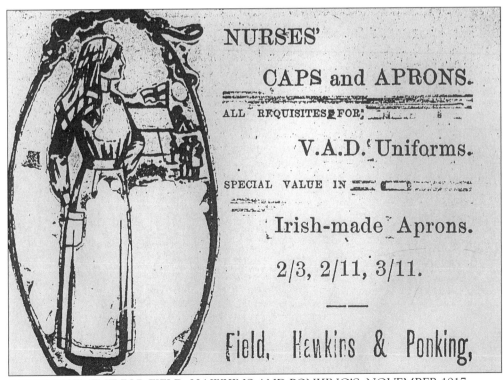

ADVERTISEMENT FOR FIELD, HAWKINS AND PONKING'S, NOVEMBER 1917.

THE BERKSHIRE YEOMANRY, 1905. The division stops off at the Market Place, on the way to its annual summer camp. This was held in the hundred acres of Newnham Murren up until the outbreak of the First World War. The Newnham camp of 1905 was particularly large, consisting of two divisions of 5,500 men apiece. On Sundays the camp was open to the public and the regimental bands played throughout the afternoon. A similar camp for a brigade of cavalry took place near Dorchester.

WALLINGFORD TOWN BAND, c. 1911.

ADVERTISEMENT FOR THE OPENING OF THE BULL CROFT, AUGUST, 1914. The Bull Croft was given to the town by Mr R.L. Powys-Lybbe. Because of the declaration of war with Germany, the celebration plans for its opening were cancelled. Whilst digging the foundations for the park keeper's lodge at the entrance, six graves were uncovered, five feet underground. The Benedictine priory of the Holy Trinity had been on this site and the coffins contained the bodies of monks who had been buried in the priory graveyard.

BULL CROFT OPENING,

Wednesday, 12th August, 1914.

The Members of the Corporation, with the Town Clerk, the Chaplain and the Borough Magistrates, will proceed from the Town Hall to the Enclosure at the Bull Croft, arriving there at 3 p.m.

The Mayor with his Mace Bearer, accompanied by the Mayoress of Reading, will arrive at the entrance at 3.15.

The Mayor of Reading, with his Mace Bearer, accompanied by the Mayoress of Wallingford, will arrive at the same time and proceed to the Enclosure.

The Members of the Corporation will be presented by the Mayor to the Mayor and Mayoress of Reading.

Miss Diana Hedges will present a bouquet to the Mayoress of Reading

The Mayor will invite the Mayor of Reading to perform the opening ceremony, and present him with a silver key.

The Deputy Mayor (Mr. Alderman Slade,) will propose a vote of thanks to the Mayor of Reading, seconded by Mr. Alderman Wells.

The Mayor of Reading will reply.

Mr. Alderman Hawkins will propose a vote of thanks to the Mayor, and request the Mayoress' acceptance of a souvenir of the occasion.

The Mayor will reply.

The Band will play "God Save the King."

THE TERRITORIALS LEAVING FOR FRANCE, AUGUST 1914. After being confined to their headquarters at the Corn Exchange overnight, they were lead by Major F. Hedges to Wallingford railway station, where they were given a send-off by over a thousand people as a violent thunderstorm raged overhead.

DRUMMER BLISSET, TERRITORIALS, 1913. Killed in action in 1916, aged 19.

CECIL WILLIAM WILSON. Killed in action in 1917. Wallingfordians had fought in many of the wars of the nineteenth century, for example 'Waterloo' Hedges, who lost a leg at the battle of Waterloo, Benjamin Massey, who was wounded at the battle of Alma (and was later decorated by Queen Victoria), H. Mapson, who fought in the Sudan, and Giles Preater who died in the Boer War. With a large empire to police, there was a constant need for men and Wallingfordians were always ready to answer their country's call.

VICTORY CARNIVAL, 1919. The peace treaty was not actually signed until the 28 June 1919 and this celebration was held on the 18 July. Over 5,000 people crowded into the Market Place to see the peace carnival before it began its procession around the town. The decorated cars, prams and people in fancy dress competed for prizes. Amongst the winners were 'allies' Miss Honeybone, 'Hiawatha' Percy Turner and 'ancient Briton' Arthur Jenkins.

THIRD-PRIZE WINNERS, VICTORY CARNIVAL, 1919.

ENTRY FOR VICTORY CARNIVAL, 1919. It was a strange coincidence that, on the day the Territorials left Wallingford for France in 1914 there was a thunderstorm, as there was during the victory carnival in 1919. This photograph was taken in Wood Street outside no. 11, where Mrs Park resided, next door to Suffolk House, where the widow of Henry Wilder lived. Woodlea, the home of George Frederick Slade, was the next house along the street.

THE WAR MEMORIAL. The war memorial was unveiled on Sunday 22 May 1921. It had been originally intended to move the drinking fountain to the Bull Croft and put the obelisk in its place but, at the last minute, it was decided to move the obelisk to the Bull Croft. The memorial was unveiled by the Lord Lieutenant of Berkshire, Herbert Benyon, and was designed by Mr Guy Dawber.

ARMISTICE DAY, c. 1932. Major Douglas Gale placing a wreath on the war memorial. Major Gale was the commanding officer of 'B' Company, 4th Battalion, Royal Berks Territorials and was related to Mr Gale of Franklin and Gale's auctioneers.

BRITISH LEGION TENTH ANNIVERSARY, 1931. The procession included the Wallingford and the Cholsey British Legion units, Cholsey brass band, the local Territorials (commanded by Sergeant W. Field), girl guides, boy scouts, Mayor Thomas Edward Wells and the members of the town council. The Cholsey British Legion banner is the one on the left-hand side.

ARMISTICE DAY PARADE, CROFT ROAD, *c.* 1936. The parade is seen here passing the tannery. One of the boy scouts is Alec Beale, who was badly wounded during the retreat to Dunkirk in 1940. He was supported then, as his condition worsened, carried by his platoon sergeant for three days. Finally, on the outskirts of Dunkirk, Alec succumbed to his wounds and it was only then that his sergeant left him. During 1970, in a quiet British cemetery near Dunkirk, their paths crossed once again.

THE WALLINGFORD TERRITORIALS, CHURN, *c.* 1938. The Bren gun crew are wearing gas masks and are practicing firing at aircraft. The man firing the weapon is Sergeant C.D. Beasley.

WALLINGFORD TERRITORIALS, RELAXING AT CAMP, *c.* 1938. The man in the back row on the left is Harry Edwards. In the front row, on the left, are George Strudwick and Snowy Whichello, whilst Freddie Spooner is at the end of the row.

ADVERTISEMENT, JANUARY 1939. Advertisements like this one in the *Berks and Oxon Advertiser* were appearing in newspapers nationally at this time. During March 1940, classes in how to deal with incendiary bombs were held in Cholsey village hall and lectures for wardens were given at the grammar school, under the supervision of Lt.- Col. A.D. Cornish.

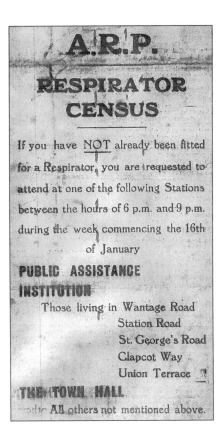

A.R.P.
RESPIRATOR CENSUS

If you have **NOT** already been fitted for a Respirator, you are requested to attend at one of the following Stations between the hours of 6 p.m. and 9 p.m. during the week commencing the 16th of January

PUBLIC ASSISTANCE INSTITUTION
Those living in Wantage Road
Station Road
St. George's Road
Clapcot Way
Union Terrace

THE TOWN HALL
All others not mentioned above.

SNOWY WHICHELLO, *c.* 1938. This photograph shows Snowy in the uniform of the Royal Berkshire Regiment. He was from Brigthwell and went to France in October 1939. He was evacuated from Dunkirk in 1940 and was killed in 1941 by a bomb blast, as was Fred Lovegrove, whilst entering an air raid shelter in Bristol.

BASIL BARCHAM, *c.* 1943. Basil was called up in 1940 and went to Malaya with the Second Battalion of the Royal Berkshires. He later volunteered for the Chindits, with whom he was mentioned in dispatches, before being invalided by sunstroke and heat exhaustion, the scars of which stayed with him for the rest of his life.

P.C. ERIC HOLLOWAY GREETING TWO AMERICAN SERVICEMEN, 1944. The soldiers were probably stationed at Howbery Park, with the American Engineers. Local children were often invited to Christmas Parties given by the USA contingent at Howbery. On several occasions the Crowmarsh Parish Council had to deal with complaints about the excessive noise coming from the servicemen's radiograms.

Nine

High Society

Royal Berkshire Horticultural Society,
(Established at WALLINGFORD, 1831,)
UNDER THE ILLUSTRIOUS PATRONAGE OF
HER MOST GRACIOUS MAJESTY the QUEEN,
Her Most Excellent Majesty the Queen Dowager, and
Her Royal Highness the Duchess of Kent.

THE SHOWS for this season will take place
(by the kind permission of W. S. BLACKSTONE, ESQ.
M.P.) in the Castle Grounds, WALLINGFORD, on
the following days, viz :—

1st Show, Thursday, May 24th.
2nd Show, Wednesday, June 13th.
3rd Show, Wednesday, July 25th.
4th Show, Tuesday, September 11th.

Members' Admission Tickets may be had of Mr. Sher-
wood, Assistant Secretary, High-street, or of Mr. T.
Lovelock at the entrance to the Grounds; and public
admission Tickets (1s. each) may be had at Mr. Payne's
Library, and the Printing Office.

By order of the Committee,
JOHN JOSEPH ALLNATT, } Honorary
JOHN KIRBY HEDGES, } Secretaries.
Wallingford, 1st May, 1838.

ADVERTISEMENT, 1838. This comes from the 4 May edition of the *Oxford Chronicle*. It is interesting to note that the Castle Grounds, at the time this advertisement went to press, belonged to William Blackstone, the Member of Parliament for Wallingford.

WEDDING OF ROSEMARY HEDGES, 1937. With her in the landau, which had been used by the Castle ladies for over fifty years, is her father, Francis Hedges. The horses were lent by Mr B. Ducker of Little Stoke.

WEDDING OF ROSEMARY HEDGES AND ALFRED WELLS, 1937. This picture shows the arrival of some of the guests. Dr George McMullan walks behind his wife and daughter. His daughter, the woman wearing the light-coloured dress, later married Dr Wilkinson.

WEDDING OF ROSEMARY HEDGES AND ALFRED WELLS, 1937. More guests arriving for the wedding. The groom's great-uncle was Edward Wells, Member of Parliament for Wallingford in the 1880s. Sadly, Captain Wells was killed in action during the retreat to Dunkirk in 1940. Large numbers of spectators lined the pavements around St Mary's church to watch the wedding.

WEDDING RECEPTION OF ROSEMARY HEDGES AND ALFRED WELLS, 1937. The bride and groom return to the Castle for the wedding reception, where the band of the Royal Berkshire Regiment played. Later they left for a honeymoon in Scotland.

HOWBERY PARK, *c.* 1906. The house was owned at this time by Havey du Cros, Member of Parliament for Hastings and a director of the Dunlop Rubber Company. He improved the house and grounds by building a new boathouse, extending the conservatory and adding a patio and patio doors to the library. A number of statues were erected in the grounds – the base of one of these has recently been found buried in the shrubbery. The covered area collapsed in 1918 and the conservatory was demolished in 1968.

HILDA GEORGIANA FABER, LADY WITTENHAM, 1912. This photograph was taken on the occasion of her fortieth birthday in Cannes. Lady Wittenham was the wife of George Denison Faber, the owner of Howbery Park from 1920 until his death in 1931. She inherited the house and retained ownership until her death in 1943. In 1931 she put the house on the market, with a reserve price of £9,000. Lord Nuffield, founder of the Morris Motor Company, was interested, but thought it too expensive.

ORNAMENTAL CANAL, NORTH BOUNDARY OF HOWBERY PARK, *c.* 1906. This feature was mentioned in a sale catalogue of 1789. This photograph was taken just after Harvey du Cros had refurbished the canal. Today, the sides of the canal have collapsed and it is full of rotting leaves and dead trees.

THE BOATHOUSE, HOWBERY PARK, *c.* 1906. This was built in 1903 by Wheelers of Reading for Harvey du Cros. During the Second World War, when the site was occupied by Canadian and American Engineers, the boathouse was allowed to become a ruin, but in recent years has been refurbished by the Hydraulics Research Company, the present owners of the site.

FRANCIS HEDGES AND FAMILY, c. 1950. Pamela is on the left, then Rosemary, Francis, Nesta, John and Diana. The photograph was taken at the rear of Castle House by Howard Evans.

Acknowledgments

The compilation of this, my second book of Wallingford photographs, would not have been possible without the help, generosity and encouragement of many people. I would like to thank the following:

First of all my wife, Ann, who allowed a bedroom to be covered in photographs and newspaper cuttings, seemingly from floor to ceiling! All the jobs I have avoided, I will now do... Many thanks to Judy Dewey for her constant encouragement, Brian Tilly and Ray Coles for their help in naming the people in the photographs, the late Olive Robinson, John Atwell, Mrs Atkins, Janet Anderson, Peter Hoddinott, Carol Chedsey, Derek Packman, Jill Toft and Lewi Reed. A special mention must go to Tony Crabbe, a friend and rival collector of Wallingford postcards, and my mother who can remember yesterday better than today. Finally I would like to mention the staff of the Centre of Oxfordshire Studies – thank you for your help and patience.